Plunkett's Pictures of Norwich and Norfolk

First published 2007
Second Edition published 2008

ISBN 10: 095532341X
ISBN 13: 9780955323416

Cover photographs:
Top: Construction of City Hall Clock Tower, 1938.
Bottom: Looking west from the top of the Cathedral Spire

Back cover photograph:
Fishing fleet from the Haven Bridge, 1933.

Published by
Grey's Publishing,
4, Fifer's Lane,
Old Catton,
Norfolk. NR6 7AF
greyspublishing@btinternet.com

Printed by Broadland Digital,
Unit 1, Vulcan House,
Vulcan Road North,
Norwich. NR6 6AQ

Contents

Norwich Castle Keep

George with his sons, Philip and Jonathan.

A Life in Pictures

George Plunkett (1913-2006)

Norwich was George Plunkett's life. The study of its history and buildings was his passion.

He was born in 1913, the younger of two children to Frank and Lily Plunkett, and grew up in their rented terraced house in Pembroke Road, in the area now known as the Golden Triangle. His parents were of modest means. His father made cardboard boxes for the shoe trade, while his mother collected insurance premiums door-to-door and took in sewing and dressmaking to supplement the household income. Family finances became stretched when George's sister Ellen unfortunately became chronically ill in her teens, requiring their mother to look after her at home. After attending the Avenue Road and City of Norwich schools, he passed the School Certificate Examination at the age of fifteen but had to give up the possibility of further education and seek employment. In the months before his sixteenth birthday, he studied book-keeping and shorthand at school and started work as soon as he could. So began a happy forty-four year administrative career in the city's Public Health Department in Churchman House, St Giles' Street. (See photograph on p82)

Ready for work: George Plunkett at 19

Despite a five-and-a-half day working week, there was luckily still time to develop new interests. In 1931 George acquired a box camera and started taking snaps around the city of the buildings and scenes that interested him. Learning to process and print his own films, he soon realised the need for better equipment and persuaded his father to buy an Ensign Carbine No 7 folding camera for his nineteenth birthday. At £5:15/- (£5.75) this represented almost a month's wages, so the camera was handled carefully. So much so, it would last three-quarters of a century and capture over 8,500 images.

By today's standards, the camera was hard to use: no zoom lens, no flash-gun, no auto-focus, no light-meter and rather crude view-finders. All exposures were a matter of judgement concerning the level of light. Although assisted by a book of complicated tables relating to type of film, latitude, month, time of day, cloud condition, shading and so forth, more often than not he would simply use his experience: "a twenty-fifth at f5.6, I think". Focusing the camera required measuring distances and for close subjects was often done by counting paces.

A very unusual feature of the camera that he found useful was its 'rising front'. This allowed the lens to be ratcheted upwards so that rooftops could be included without tilting the camera; he did not want buildings to look as if they were falling over backwards.

If a picture came out badly he could usually retake it another day, but not always, as there was redevelopment constantly on the go. In the 1920s and 30s the slum clearance programme was responsible for the demolition of countless crumbling old tenements and courtyards in the city centre, while the population moved out to the expanding new suburbs. George consequently set himself the task, before it was too late, of creating a photographic survey of the buildings that remained.

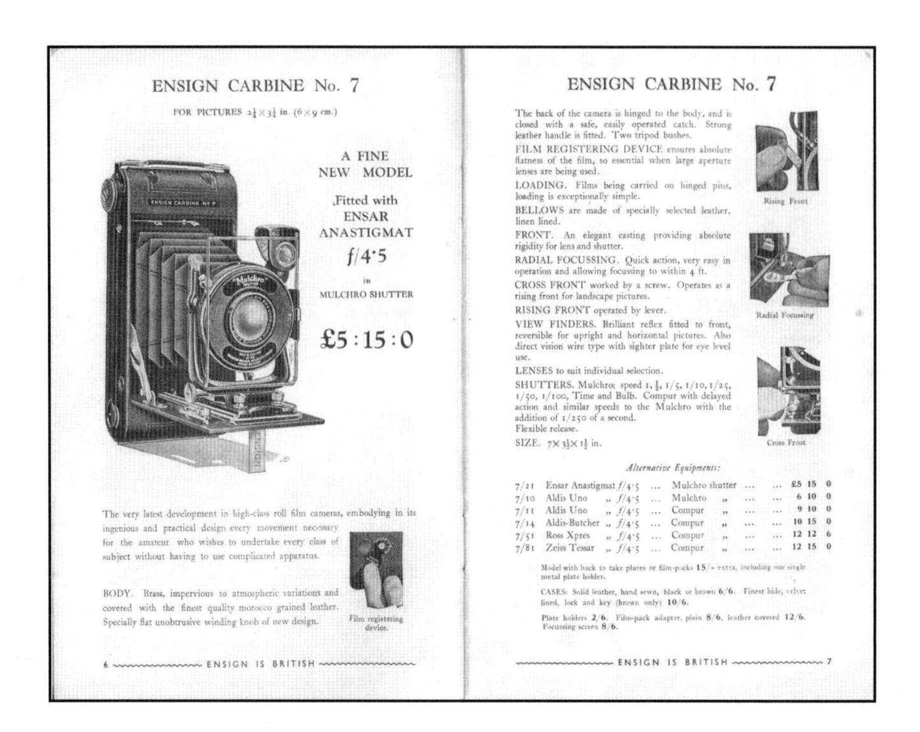

ENSIGN CARBINE No. 7

FOR PICTURES $2\frac{1}{4} \times 3\frac{1}{4}$ in. (6 × 9 cm.)

A FINE NEW MODEL

Fitted with ENSAR ANASTIGMAT f/4·5 in MULCHRO SHUTTER

£5 : 15 : 0

The very latest development in high-class roll film cameras, embodying in its ingenious and practical design every movement necessary for the amateur who wishes to undertake every class of subject without having to use complicated apparatus.

BODY. Brass, impervious to atmospheric variations and covered with the finest quality morocco grained leather. Specially flat unobtrusive winding knob of new design.

Film registering device.

6 ENSIGN IS BRITISH

ENSIGN CARBINE No. 7

The back of the camera is hinged to the body, and is closed with a safe, easily operated catch. Strong leather handle is fitted. Two tripod bushes.

FILM REGISTERING DEVICE ensures absolute flatness of the film, so essential when large aperture lenses are being used.

LOADING. Films being carried on hinged pins, loading is exceptionally simple.

BELLOWS are made of specially selected leather, linen lined.

FRONT. An elegant casting providing absolute rigidity for lens and shutter.

RADIAL FOCUSSING. Quick action, very easy in operation and allowing focussing to within 4 ft.

CROSS FRONT worked by a screw. Operates as a rising front for landscape pictures.

RISING FRONT operated by lever.

VIEW FINDERS. Brilliant reflex fitted to front, reversible for upright and horizontal pictures. Also direct vision wire type with sighter plate for eye level use.

LENSES to suit individual selection.

SHUTTERS. Mulchro: speed 1, ½, 1/5, 1/10, 1/25, 1/50, 1/100, Time and Bulb. Compur with delayed action and similar speeds to the Mulchro with the addition of 1/250 of a second.
Flexible release.

SIZE. $7 \times 3\frac{1}{2} \times 1\frac{1}{2}$ in.

Rising Front

Radial Focussing

Cross Front

Alternative Equipments:

7/21	Ensar Anastigmat f/4·5	Mulchro shutter	£5	15	0
7/10	Aldis Uno „ f/4·5	Mulchro „	6	10	0
7/11	Aldis Uno „ f/4·5	Compur „	9	10	0
7/14	Aldis-Butcher „ f/4·5	Compur „	10	15	0
7/51	Ross Xpres „ f/4·5	Compur „	12	12	6
7/81	Zeiss Tessar „ f/4·5	Compur „	12	15	0

Model with back to take plates or film-packs **15/-** extra, including one single metal plate holder.

CASES: Solid leather, hand sewn, black or brown **6/6**. Finest hide, velvet lined, lock and key (brown only) **10/6**.

Plate holders **2/6**. Film-pack adapter, plain **8/6**, leather covered **12/6**. Focussing screen **8/6**.

ENSIGN IS BRITISH 7

The Advert for the Ensign Carbine No 7

Details of every picture taken were carefully written into a register. The records show how he would proceed along a street photographing buildings in turn, sometimes shooting a roll of film in as little as ten minutes. Developing and printing it in the blacked-out kitchen back home took a little longer.

He took a few experimental photos on 'Dufay' colour transparency film but preferred black-and-white as he was able to do the processing and make prints himself. These he put into albums, arranging them by category such as river bridges, the city walls, the tram system, cinemas, industrial architecture and so forth, or else alphabetically by street name.

Occasionally his bike carried him beyond the city boundaries, there, usually, to photograph village churches. Anywhere within a 12-mile radius was considered fair game for a half-day expedition with his Bartholomew map, folding camera, tripod and puncture-repair kit on board. Despite visiting so many ecclesiastical buildings, he never felt the urge to attend their services, preferring to admire the works of man.

His favourite style of church architecture was Norman, with its decorative doorways. For domestic buildings, Georgian was his fascination and Norwich had an abundance of examples to keep his camera busy during the 1930s. By the end of that decade when he was called up to serve in the RAF, George had already achieved over half his lifetime's output of photographs.

World War Two necessarily interrupted his career and photography. During his first two years in uniform, his mission, with dummy lights and fires, was to try to mislead night-time enemy planes into dropping their bombs harmlessly onto the Leicestershire countryside rather than factories and houses. Having had little success however, he was temporarily seconded to New Romney in Kent to set up a dummy airfield with model planes and fake runway lighting, again to try to divert German fire away from the real thing. It was while returning from there that, much to his alarm, he got the enemy's full attention when a Focke-Wulf 190 began raking his two-coach train with cannon-fire. He threw himself on the floor of the carriage and took cover under his kit-bag as best he could but with remarkable irony the steam-locomotive's boiler exploded after being hit by a shell, its flying debris in turn striking and bringing down the fighter, killing its pilot.

Soon after that episode, George was sent overseas to Algeria, Tunisia and Italy with the 255 Night Fighter Squadron. This time he was using his runway-lighting skills to create real air-strips rather than dummies. When the fighting was over, he was posted to No. 6 Base Personnel Office in Portici, near Naples, for clerical duties and reached the rank of Corporal. There, he developed a love of opera, attending many performances at the San Carlo Opera House and had time for sight-seeing around Pompeii, Herculaneum, Capri and Rome. Being without his camera, he used pen and paper to record the local architecture.

George serving in Portici during World War Two.

After being demobbed in 1946, he returned to Norwich, resuming work at the Health Department and catching up with photography of the Blitz's after-effects. The following year he was elected to the council of the Norfolk and Norwich Archaeological Society, having been a member since he was twenty-two.

Also, in 1947, he married Margaret Harper, formerly a nurse, midwife and then a health visitor in the service of Norwich Corporation. Together they set up home in Thorpe St Andrew and raised two sons. About this time he traced records of his ancestry back to the early nineteenth century in the parish registers of St Martin at Oak, Norwich, and a century earlier eight miles away in the town of Wymondham.

In the 1960s, George and his family lived in College Road, his sons going to the same schools that he had, forty years previously. Meanwhile, his camera recorded more dramatic changes to the city centre: the widening of St Stephen's Street, the construction of Anglia Square, and the contentious creation of the inner link road. He particularly resented the destruction of historic buildings and sections of the city wall to make way for the new roads and flyover.

Fearing that their own neighbourhood off Earlham Road was going downhill, with houses being converted to flats and let out to rowdy students, the family moved back to quieter Thorpe. Between retiring from local government in 1973 and reaching state pension age, George took a job working with similar congenial "oldies" at Norwich Union's Head Office in the city centre.

About this time, the family acquired its first car – a Mini. This allowed tours of the county's far corners, to photograph Norfolk's six hundred plus mediaeval parish churches. Although he didn't drive, his wife Margaret had been sitting behind the wheel of her father's car since the age of twelve and had obtained a licence in the days before any form of test was necessary.

In 1987, George's first book Disappearing Norwich was published, illustrated by his own photographs of sights and scenes that had subsequently been lost. Three years later Rambles in Old Norwich joined it, giving the history of some of the city's lesser-known remaining buildings.

Following his wife's sudden passing in 1990, George continued to pursue his interest in local history with undiminished vigour. Every day the Evening News would be carefully read, and articles relating to the city's history or development added to his press-cuttings books. Ultimately these would come to occupy 12 feet of shelf space, and together with a card-index that he maintained for it, form a very useful and convenient resource. It was not all one way as he himself contributed articles, photographs and letters several times a year to the newspaper.

In 1996 the Norfolk and Norwich Archaeological Society celebrated its 150th anniversary. At a tea party in Suckling Hall, a surprise presentation to mark his 'long and distinguished service to the society' was made to him of a commemorative paperweight inscribed with his name. Over the years, he'd had several papers published: Old Norwich Doorways (1942); 17th Century Ceiling at 12 St Stephen's Street, Norwich (1944); St George (Middle) Street, Norwich – In Memoriam (1970); Churchman House, St Giles' Street, Norwich (1975); and Norfolk Church Screens (1865 Survey) (1979). He was particularly well qualified to write the article on Churchman House, having worked within its walls for almost half a century.

In 2000, George's photographs of the city were placed on the world-wide-web, his site generating a steady stream of appreciative messages and enquiries from visitors around the world. He was always pleased to help, and although getting less sprightly with age, his memory didn't fail.

In the end, perhaps both he and his camera had lasted longer than he would have imagined when he took his first pictures as a young man. Those early negatives are still in as good a condition and are as usable as ever. Will today's photographs on digital memory cards and discs last for seventy - five years? With a little care, let's hope so.

Jonathan Plunkett, 2007.

His faithful friend: the camera that George used for so many years to capture Norwich.

Scenes of a City Celebrating - a Jubilee and a Coronation

The 1930s were an eventful time for the people of Great Britain, particularly the Royal family. 1935 was the Silver Jubilee year of King George V and Queen Mary and the city joined in the celebrations. A competition was held to find the best decorated buildings or street and **Jarrolds, above**, won the third prize.

Another entrant was **Rampant Horse Street**, shown here, looking toward St Stephen's Street.

The Royal Hotel at the top of Prince of Wales Road looked even more majestic than usual.

London Street, seen **above** from Bank Plain, shared its honours with
Prince of Wales Road, below, a right royal street!

Left: The Royal Arcade flies the British flag.

Below: Magdalen Street. Notice the well-known city shop, Loose's, who were "Importers & Exporters, Specialists in China, Glass & Earthen Wares."

Above: On the 6th May, 1935, the official day for celebrating the Jubilee, crowds gathered near Britannia Barracks, on Mousehold Heath. They watched a **Review of the Troops**, conducted by the Lord Lieutenant of Norfolk, Russell J. Colman.

Below: Trams ran up and down **Gurney Road**, transporting the public to and from the city.

The Coronation of King George VI, in 1937, came only two years after the Silver Jubilee. After an unsettling period, due to the abdication crisis, the city once again entered into the spirit of the celebrations. The decorations in **St Giles'**, left, won Highly Commended in a competition similar to the one held for the Jubilee. Private homes were decorated too, as **104, Chapel Field Road**, standing in the shadows of Caley's Factory, shows **below**.

The Market Place, cleared of all stalls in preparations for the festivities

Messrs Green's store and the entrance to **Orford Place**.

Orford Place won a second prize for its street decorations. In the middle of the picture you can see the Tramway Shelter and Timekeeper's Office that was built in 1928, at a cost of £650.

St Benedict's Street.

Right: Charing Cross

Below: C.J Howard, the game dealers, on **Fyebridge Street**, won a Highly Commended award from the judges.

Left: The houses in **Rose Yard**, off St Augustine's Street, received a special mention from the judges. Whatever must the little girl in the picture thought of it all?

Below: A beacon bonfire was built by boy scouts on **Mousehold Heath**. They made use of materials from the Norwich slum-clearances that took place in the 1930s.

Norwich in the 1930s and 40s

Norwich underwent a lot of changes during the 1930s and 40s.
The Market Place and Municipal buildings were redeveloped whilst
the Second World War meant that Norwich's most historic buildings had to
be protected from the bombs, which inevitably arrived and caused great damage.

Above: The **City Hall** and its clock tower radically changed the skyline of Norwich.

Bacon House, Colegate. This Elizabethan timber framed property was built by Henry Bacon, who was Mayor and Sheriff of Norwich in the 16th century. The Duke of Northumberland visited here on his way to challenge Kett's men. In the early 20th century it was restored by Norwich antiquary, Walter Rye.

Left: The Octagon Chapel was built for the Presbyterians between 1754 and 1756. It was designed by the local architect, Thomas Ivory. John Wesley described it as "the most elegant meeting house in Europe."

Elm Hill is, today, one of Norwich's most treasured streets. It was saved from demolition in 1927 by the Norwich Society, which continues to play a vital role in the preservation of Norwich's historical buildings.

Left: No 12-16, Elm Hill.

Below: 21-27, Elm Hill. Notice the faded writing on the building which says "Ye Olde Curiosity Shoppe."

Fyebridge is considered to be the site of the earliest bridge in the city, dating from the 12th century. In 1932 work on the current bridge was begun. It was a mammoth task and the photo **above**, taken from Roache's Court, Elm Hill, shows the dredger involved in its construction. **Below**, the bridge's carriageway open to traffic in 1934.

Fyebridge Street runs into **Magdalen Street, above**. The tram lines running along the road were for the route which went from Unthank Road, through the city, out along Magdalen Street and terminated at Denmark Road.

Right: 44-48, Magdalen Street.
Smith & Sons were wholesale and retail druggists trading from this 18th century merchant's house.

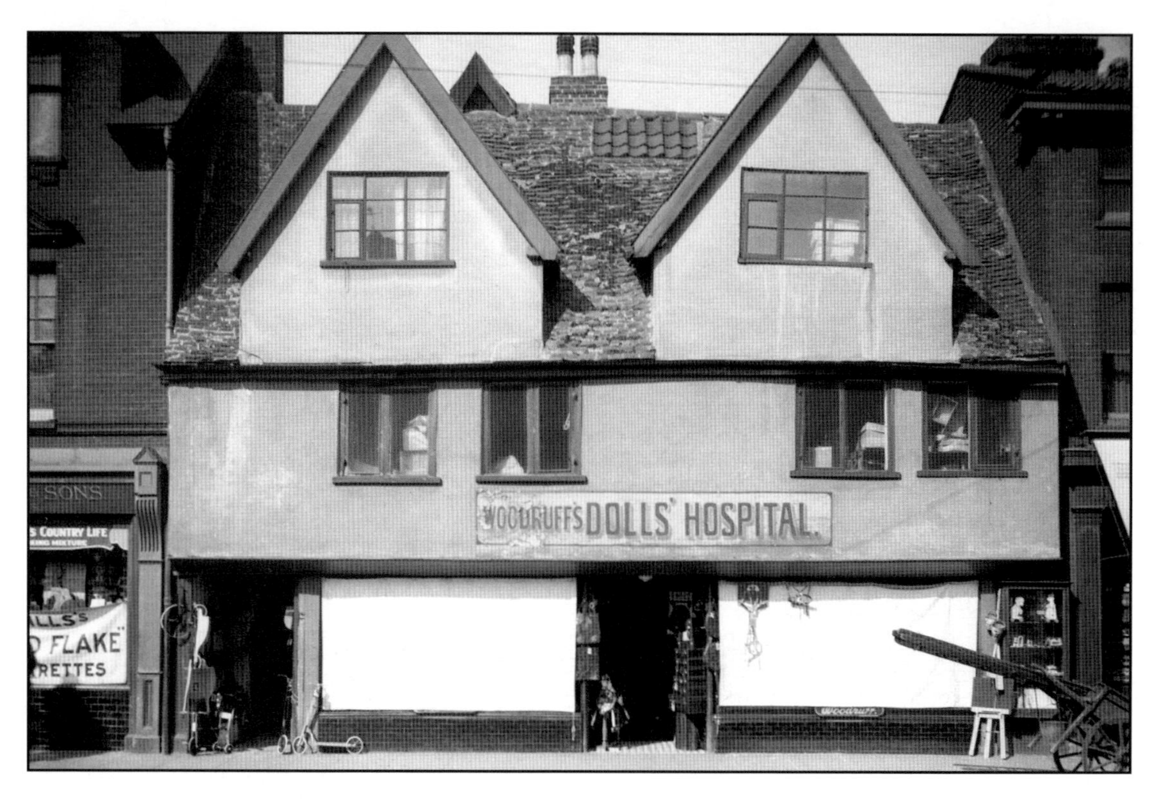

Above: Woodruff's Dolls' Hospital in Magdalen Street

Left: 35-39, St Augustine's Street - Magdalen Street's neighbour, looking more prosperous than it does today.

The shops that can be seen are A.J Woods, the monumental masons and R.J Bales, a fruiterer. The Prince of Wales Public House is at the far left.

The Maddermarket Theatre. Initially a Roman Catholic Chapel, it became the home and theatre of Nugent Monck's Norwich Players in 1921, where they attempted to recreate an Elizabethan theatre.

Stranger's Hall. The mainly 15th century merchant's home was saved from falling into ruin by Leonard Bolingbroke in 1899. He restored it and gave it to the city in 1922. The folk museum he started has continued into the present day. At the time of this photograph, a Mr Leney was the curator.

Right: This 14th century flint wall was part of the home of William Appleyard, the first mayor of Norwich in the early 15th century. The building went on to be used as a workhouse and was known as **“The Bridewell.”** In the 1930s it was the “Bridewell Museum of Local Industries” and continues in a similar role today.

Left: No 25, Bedford Street. Behind the rugs hanging out of the windows is the name of a popular local shop, Hovells. The family business was started in 1864. After nearly one hundred and forty years on the corner of Bedford Street and Bridewell Alley, the business moved to new premises on the outskirts of the city.

Left: Exchange Street and another local landmark - **Jarrold's**. The grand building attached to the shop was the Norwich Corn Exchange. It was opened in 1863 and demolished in 1964. Jarrold's built an extension on the site which was opened, a year later, in 1965.

Below: Although on Guildhall Hill, this building was known as **No1, The Market Place**. On the left of the picture is Lower Goat Lane and the opening to the right of Moy's Coal Order Office leads to Labour in Vain Yard.

Above: This tin hut in the Market Place was the **Police Office and Drill Hall**.

Left: The Estates Department, the Market Place. The building on the left was originally the Black Prince Tavern and the building on the right was the Wellington Tavern; just two of the many pubs that the Market Place used to have.

Above: The Municipal Offices for the City Council. The right block was originally the Oxford Hotel but was bought by the Corporation in 1876. The remaining parts were subsequently bought and used for the Town Clerk's Department, the City Engineer's Department and the Estate Surveyor's Department. However, due to the ever increasing duties of local government it was decided that more space was needed. So, the Municipal Offices were demolished, and a new **City Hall** was built, seen behind the remains of the old Municipal Offices, **below**.

Whilst the City Hall was being built, the **Market Place** was reconstructed too. Many of the buildings in the picture, **above**, were cleared away during the work, shown **below**.

While work on the Market Place was being carried out, a temporary **Provisions Market** was set up in the courtyard of City Hall. It became known as "the Sand Pit."

The Garden of Remembrance was laid out roughly where the Municipal Offices used to stand. It was built in remembrance of the sons of Norwich who died in World War One.

Left: The Royal Arcade was designed by local architect, George Skipper and built in 1899 on the site of the Royal Hotel. The front of the hotel, dated to 1846, was incorporated into the entrance to the Arcade.

Right: Gentlemen's Walk was so called because it was traditionally the fashionable place for the "man about town" to stroll. In the 1930s it was a popular shopping street, as it continues to be today. To enable people to walk along "The Walk" with more ease, the street was pedestrianised in the 1980s.

Above: 19-23, The Haymarket.
On the corner is one of the twelve branches of F. Lambert and Son Ltd, who sold tea and tobacco in the city. Above the shop was the Mecca Café. Today the building serves a similar purpose as a branch of popular coffee shop chain Starbucks.

Left: 34-36, The Market Place.
The building on the right is the Sir Garnet Wolseley Pub. This is one of the few buildings that survived the Market Place reconstruction.

Right: Norwich had so many inns and pubs that it even has a street known as **Back of the Inns**. It seems like healthy eating isn't completely a 21st century obsession - note the Golden Health Stores Ltd.

Below: The Haymarket. In June 1937, whilst being driven to market, these cows escaped from Orford Hill and made their way to see Sir Thomas Browne's statue. As the crowds surrounding them show, they were quite a spectacle!

Left: 15th century **St Peter Mancroft** is one of the most magnificent churches in Norwich. The tower, seen here from St Peter's Street, is almost one hundred and fifty feet high. The buildings in the front right of the picture, on St Peter's Street, were demolished when the City Hall was built.

Below: These buildings on **Bethel Street** were demolished to make way for the new Fire Station.

Right: The tower of **St Peter Mancroft**, seen from **Bethel Street**. These shops were trading from the former stables of the Wheatsheaf Pub.

Below: The Morning Star Pub on the corner of St. Gregory's Alley and Pottergate.

Left: Lower Goat Lane which runs parallel to Upper Goat Lane.

Below: The east wing of a medieval house in **Ninham's Court**, which is named after Henry Ninham, a Norwich artist who lived here and produced a series of sketches of the city gates.

Left: The Hippodrome, St Giles' Street. This building had a varied history, starting life as a Grand Opera House in 1903. It became a Music Hall but by 1930 it had changed again, to a cinema. On the night that this photograph was taken, "Morgenrot" was showing. According to the illuminated banner it was a film that "London was afraid to show!"

Below: 6-14, St Giles' Street, looking towards the city. The trams running along here took people between Thorpe and Earlham Road.

Right: 41-43, St Giles' Street. The Education and Treasurer's Department, formerly insurance offices, was designed by George Skipper.

Below: Before the Inner Link Road, this is where **Grapes Hill, Unthank Road** and **St Giles'** met. The photograph shows the electric tramway lines being renewed in 1933.

The front of the **Theatre Royal** after a fire, which broke out near the stage.
A new theatre was built and opened in September 1935.

The Assembly House, seen here in 1935, before it was restored by Norwich shoe manufacturer, Henry Sexton and given to the city. Since the 18th century, it has played a prominent role in the city as a meeting place for the people of Norwich.

The Boar's Head Inn stood on the corner of Surrey Street and St Stephen's Street. The thatched building was bombed in the Second World War and had to be demolished, but a new building was built on the site and given the same name.

Norwich Union General Buildings on Surrey Street. The Eastern Counties Omnibus Company building had recently been opened in 1936 and cost £50000 to build.

Right: Surrey House, the Head Office of Norwich Union. It was designed by George Skipper and built in 1901. As well as its neo-classical exterior, it is well known for the "Marble Hall" inside.

Below: All Saints' Green, with a bus coming up Westlegate. The Tuns was one of many Steward and Patteson pubs in the city.

Left: The Royal Army Barracks on All Saints' Green were built in 1771-2 and designed by Thomas Ivory, who was also the architect of the Assembly Rooms and the original Theatre.
In the 1930s the barracks were the headquarters of, among others, the Royal Army Medical Corps, the Cadet Norfolk Artillery and the 84th East Anglian Field Brigade.

Below: 21, All Saints' Green.
This building was initially an Assembly Rooms. It then became part of Bonds, which had numbers 9, 13,15, 17, 19, 21 and 23 of Ber Street. The "Restaurant, Ball Room and Furnishing Hall" has since become part of the John Lewis chain.

Golden Ball Street meeting Ber Street, opposite St John the Baptist Church on Timberhill. Golden Ball Street was named after a pub that stood on this road.

The Bell Hotel was originally a coaching inn. In the 18th Century it was the home of the Hell-Fire club, a group of raucous young men who caused trouble for Methodist preachers who came to the Tabernacle on Timberhill.

Looking west from the Castle Mound with **Castle Meadow** in the forefront of the picture. Boots, the Chemist, is still in the same place as it is shown here.

A closer look at **Castle Meadow**. Both A.E Coe & Sons and Ponds are still trading from Castle Meadow.

Above: The Norfolk and Norwich Agricultural Hall. Built in 1882, it was temporarily used as a repertory theatre in the mid 1930s. The illuminated posters tell us that “Other Men’s Wives” was showing and that it cost 2/6 to see it.

Left: The Head Post Office. This was originally the Crown Bank, built in 1866. The bank closed in 1870 when one of its bankers, Robert Harvey, shot himself after losing a lot of the bank’s money.

Above: Bank Plain. At number 15 was J. Bloomfield, the antique dealer. Spelmans, the land agents can also be seen at number 17.

Right: St Andrew's Hill, looking towards St Andrew's Hall.

Above: Suckling Hall. Although parts of the building date from the 14th century, it was named after the Suckling family who lived here in the 16th century. Ethel Colman, the first female mayor in the country, and her sister, Helen, restored it and presented it to the city in 1924. In more recent years it has been home to the independent Cinema City.

Left: Garsett House was built in the late 16th century, by Robert Garsett, the Sheriff of Norwich in 1599. Timbers that supposedly came from the wrecked Armada were used in the construction. The house was truncated when tram routes were laid on St Andrew's Street. In the 1930s Ernest A. Kent ran his law practice here. On his death, he bequeathed the building to the Norfolk and Norwich Archaeological Society.

Above: 8-12, Princes Street, looking toward St Peter Hungate Church and the top of Elm Hill. Notice the advertising for popular brands, Cadbury's and Wall's Ice cream, on the front of the shop.

Right: 8 and 9, Tombland. Number 9 is a newsagent's. One wonders what the headlines on 5th July, 1936 were!

Left: 4-6, Tombland

Below: St Ethelbert's House, Tombland. Although a Georgian building, it was extensively altered during the Victorian period. In the 1930s it was W.Boswell and Son Antiques. The building was later used as a bar, appropriately called Boswell's.

The Maid's Head Hotel is one of the oldest inns in Norwich, possibly dating back to 1287. It was referred to in the Paston letters written during the 15th century. The building was restored in the 1890s by Walter Rye, a Norwich antiquarian and mayor.

1-4 St Martin's Palace Plain. The building on the corner is the car dealership, Bussey and Sabberton Brothers Ltd. Busseys is still the leading Ford dealer in the area.

Left: The Adam and Eve pub. Believed to date from the 13th Century, it probably served men working on the Cathedral. Seven centuries on, it remains a popular pub and its history makes it an unofficial tourist site.

Below: These offices are a part of the complex of buildings at the **Great Hospital**, which was founded in 1249 by Walter de Suffield, the Bishop of Norwich, to look after the needy of Norwich. It serves a similar purpose today, by providing residential care for the older generation of Norwich citizens.

Right: The Erpingham Gate is the western entrance to the Cathedral. It was built in the 15th century, in remembrance of Sir Thomas Erpingham, a Norwich man who fought at Agincourt. He was immortalised by Shakespeare in Henry V.

Left: The west front of the **Cathedral** after it had been cleaned.

The Norwich Cathedral Cloisters were built between the 13th and 15th centuries.

Left: The Eastern Walk looking south.

Below: The Cloister Garth.

Above: 8-12, The Cathedral Close.

Right: 50, The Cathedral Close. In this home on Hook's Walk, from 1792 to 1817, Dr Frank Sayers, the poet, physician, essayist, and antiquarian, lived.

Pull's Ferry, before restoration. The watergate marks where the canal was that was used to transport materials arriving by river, to the Cathedral building site. In the 19th century, the ferry house was named after the last ferryman, John Pull, who ran a pub here.

Pull's Ferry from Riverside Road. The restoration in the 1940s cost about £2000. After it was finished, it was used as the HQ of Norwich Girl Guides.

Bishop Bridge, constructed in the 14th century, looking toward The Close entrance. It is the only medieval bridge left in the city. The gate built over the westernmost arch was demolished in 1791.

Bishop Bridge, looking towards Riverside Road and the Gas Works.

13th century **Cow Tower** was built in a bend of the River Wensum, for the collection of tolls from boats. It was then used as a prison for the Cathedral until it was given to the city in 1387 and rebuilt in 1399.

Above: Cow Tower seen from the meadow of the Great Hospital.

Left: Cow Tower seen from the opposite bank of the river, where Zaks restaurant now stands.

Above: This was originally **the Norwich Yarn Factory**, built in 1836-7. It became Jarrold's Printing Works in 1902.

Left: The Eastern Boom Tower was built as part of the scheme to surround the city with defensive walls in the 14th century. Chains were stretched between the boom towers on either side of the river to prevent unwanted boats travelling any further.

Left: 5, Rose Lane; The Tudor Hall Stores. When this photograph was taken, David Playford was the proprietor of the shop and bakery, which sold "The Better Bread Supply."

Below: The Watson Dispensary on the corner of **King Street and Rose Lane**.

A remaining section of **St Benedict's Gate** and the old city wall.

The Valori Brothers, the fish merchants, and J.H Rainthorpe, the stationers, at **2, Dereham Road.**

What a difference a year makes! Numbers **5 to 7 Dereham Road, above**, were demolished and replaced by the **Regal Cinema**, between 1937 and 1938. It was closed in 1958 and has since been converted to a bar.

The Grapes Hotel, Earlham Road, was destroyed by fire in 1942.

The Tuns Inn on Unthank Road, which is still open for business but under a new name, Temple Bar.

St John the Baptist, Roman Catholic Cathedral, built between 1882 and 1910 on the site of the city gaol. The cathedral's size is illustrated as it it dwarfs the tram running along side!

The south front of **Earlham Hall**. Built in the mid 17th century, it is well-known as the home of the Gurney family, whose most famous daughter was Elizabeth Fry. The Norwich Corporation bought it in 1925 and leased it to the UEA in the 1960s, who first used it as the Administration Centre. It is now home to the University's Law School.

The Black Horse Inn on Earlham Road. The two wings have since been demolished.

The Norwich offices of the **Milk Marketing Board** on **Unthank Road**, built in 1939.

Above: The pagoda in Chapel Field Gardens. Built in 1876 and based on plans by Thomas Jeckyll, it was exhibited by Messrs Barnard, Bishop and Barnard in Paris and Philadelphia. George Plunkett's great-uncle hand forged much of the bas relief work. In 1880, a public subscription bought the pagoda for Chapel Field Gardens at a cost of £500.

Below Left: Chapel Field House on Chapel Field North, with a wrought iron balcony.

Below Right: St Mary's Croft, Chapel Field, was built in 1881 by Captain Crowe. What a lovely view this pair of houses must have over the park!

The Jolly Butchers' on Ber Street. When this photograph was taken Black Anna and her husband had recently taken over as landlord and landlady. Black Anna's infamous singing sessions would continue into the 1970s.

Prince of Wales Road, looking towards the Railway Station.

4-8 Barn Road, which has changed beyond all recognition since it became part of the Inner Link Road.

The Britannia Barracks, on Britannia Road, were opened in 1887.

Norwich during World War Two

A fortified city! Plunkett's pictures of wartime Norwich were mainly taken at the start of the hostilities, before he went to serve his country. They show the city preparing for the horrific onslaught of bombing raids that caused so much destruction.

Above: The Dark Entry of **the Cathedral Cloisters** surrounded by sandbags.

A brick surface shelter being constructed outside Bonds on **All Saints Green**.

Trenches being dug on the **Cattlemarket**.

Right: Sandbags surrounding the **Drill Hall on Chapel Fiel**d. They were put up during "The Crisis" of 1938 when it was feared that war was imminent. The Drill Hall survived the war but was demolished in 1963.

Below: A partially constructed trench in **Chapel Field Gardens**. "The Crisis" caused the gardens to close but they were reopened in 1939.

One of the most historic buildings in Norwich, **The Guildhall**, had to be protected.

Left: Measures were taken to protect the stained glass.

Below: Sandbags surrounded the building.

Trenches being dug outside Chamberlins on **Guildhall Hill**.

Sandbags surrounding a Norwich Corporation Electricity Supply Sub-Station on **Wellington Lane**.

A surface brick shelter being built in the **Haymarket**. What would Sir Thomas Browne think?

The caretaker's shelter at **Churchman House**.

Norwich during 1950s and 60s

Princess Elizabeth visited the city in 1951 to open Norwich's Festival of Britain. Thousands came to see her as she spoke from the City Hall balcony and then went on to the Castle to open the Colman Galleries. She is seen here making her way to the Assembly House for lunch with the Lord Mayor.

Barclays Bank at **Stump Cross**, where Magdalen Street *(on the right)* and Botolph Street *(on the left)* met. The whole area was redeveloped in the late Sixties and early Seventies, with the creation of Anglia Square and a flyover.

The Norwich Institute for the Blind on Magdalen Street, built in the late 19th century.

A neglected **Monastic Chapel** behind Elm Hill. It was built by Father Ignatious for his Benedictine Monks in the 1866. It was forced to close in 1876 and fell into ruin. In more recent years it has been used by the Norwich School of Art and Design.

1, Tombland at the junction with Queen Street. Plowright's, the antiques shop, is on the corner. Cars no longer drive down Queen Street as it has been pedestrianised.

7-11 Tombland. In this photograph numbers 8 and 9 serve the same purpose as they did in the 1930s picture on p49.

Norwich Gas Works in Bishopgate. Notice the hanging sign of the Adam and Eve pub, which was opposite. What a mixture of ancient and modern! The gas works were sold to the Norwich Corporation in 1972 and then demolished. The new Law Courts were built on the site.

Above: 1-7, St Martin's Palace Plain. The large Georgian building at the front right of the picture is Cotman House, where the Norwich artist, John Sell Cotman, founded an art school.

Right: The 12th century tower and the 15th century **Cathedral** spire undergoing repair in 1963 to make them safe.

The Steward and Patteson Brewery on Barrack Street, looking towards the bottom of Silver Road. In 1974, the 4.3 acre site was bought and the buildings demolished by the council, who then built new homes and offices there.

Looking up **Kett's Hill**.

Above: Prefabricated houses on **Kett's Hill**. Over five hundred were put up in Norwich in the 1940s to try to ease the housing shortage after the Second World War.

Right: Looking up **Grapes Hill**. These smart houses were demolished in preparation for the Inner Link Road, which was opened in 1971.

Looking toward **Upper St Giles'** from the corner of Willow Lane.

Churchman House, St Giles' Street. Dating from the 18th century, it has had a variety of uses. As the Public Health Department, it was, for forty-four years, George Plunkett's place of work. It is now the Norwich Registry Office.

St Giles' Street meeting Bethel Street.

The Hippodrome on St Giles' shortly before it was demolished to make way for a multi-storey car park in 1960.

Above: 1-11 Charing Cross. This narrow street has since been widened.

Left: Norwich Free Library on St Andrew's Street. Opened in 1857 as one of the earliest public libraries in the country, it was closed when the Central Library was opened on Bethel Street in 1963. The Free Library was then demolished as part of improvements made at the St Andrew's Street and Duke Street junction.

Left: The Norwich Corn Exchange, seen from Bedford Street, just before it was demolished in 1964.

Right: 2-22, Exchange Street. The "R.E" of R.E. Thorns, the "ironmongers and fireplace dealers" can just be seen on the side of the buildings at the corner of Lobster Lane. The D.I.Y. business still trades from here.

Above: The Friends' Meeting House in Upper Goat Lane. The architect was J.T Patience and it was built in 1826.

Left: The Norfolk and Norwich Subscription Library was started in 1784 in a room in St Andrew's Hall. It moved to Guildhall Hill but after one hundred and forty years it stopped loaning books for good. The building went on to be used as the Citizen Advice Bureau and is now a restaurant, fittingly called "The Library."

Norwich Central Library was opened by Queen Elizabeth, the Queen Mother, in 1963. The track at the front of the building was Lady Lane, later named Esperanto Way. This library was destroyed by a devastating fire in 1994. The Forum has now been built in its place.

Messrs. Lambert's Tea and Tobacco Warehouse, The Haymarket.
It was demolished in the 1960s and C & A was built in its place in 1969.

The Haymarket Picture House was later known as the Gaumont Cinema. It was opened in 1911, extended in 1929 and demolished in 1959. It was replaced in 1961 a Peter Robinson shop, **below**, and then became Topshop.

Right: The Eastern Entrance to the **Royal Arcade**.

Below: Davey Place, a pedestrian way leading between Gentlemen's Walk and Castle Meadow, was created in 1812. Jonathan Davey, an alderman of the city and known radical, caused trouble when he threatened to make a hole in the King's Head. He was put under house arrest. Meanwhile the King's Head Inn was sold and then demolished, on Davey's orders, to create this thoroughfare!

The Plough Public House on **Market Avenue**.

The Shire House on Market Avenue was built in 1822 and designed by William Wilkins, the younger. It was once used as the administrative centre of Norfolk. At the time this photo was taken, it was the County Court House, Shire Hall Chambers and Her Majesty's Customs and Excise Department. It is now the Royal Norfolk Regimental Museum.

Above: Bonds Department Store on All Saints Green which was erected in 1952, to replace the Bonds buildings bombed during the Second World War.

Right: The Crescent is one of Norwich Union's Offices. This striking building was constructed between 1959-62, on the corner of All Saints' Green and Surrey Street.

Curls Department Store, on the corner of Rampant Horse Street and Brigg Street, being rebuilt in 1955, after it was heavily bombed during World War Two.

St Stephen's Plain

Marks and Spencer on St Stephen's Street. The building dates to 1912 when it was opened as Bunting's Drapery store.

8-12, St Stephen's Street. These recently completed buildings were an introduction to the development that would completely change St Stephen's in the 1950s and 60s.

Left: 52-68, St Stephen's Street.
All these buildings were demolished in the St Stephen's Street re-development which was based on proposals from the City of Norwich Plan of 1945. It found that the street had "few buildings of outstanding merit" and proposed that it be provided with dual carriageways and pavements 15 feet wide. Also the new buildings were to be controlled in so far as materials, height and design were concerned.

Below: The top of **St Stephen's Street meeting Chapel Field Road**. This is approximately where St Stephen's Gate would have stood.

The Norfolk and Norwich Hospital, which was built in 1882.

1-5, St Stephen's Road before the roundabout and Inner Link Road were created.

The subway that links St Stephen's Street, Chapel Field Road and St Stephen's Road, being constructed in 1964. The new St Stephen's Street buildings can be seen.

The Volunteer Stores Public House on Chapel Field North was demolished in 1969.

66-96, Chapel Field Road. These houses were demolished when the road was widened.

Looking up **Theatre Street** from St Stephen's church. These handsome buildings were lost when the increasing numbers of cars in the city centre meant roads had to be widened.

Left: R.J. Read Ltd's Flour Mill was built in 1837 as the Albion Spinning Mill. Silk, worsted and mohair were produced here. It became a flour mill in 1934. It has recently been converted into flats.

Below: The Norfolk Club - a private members club on Upper King Street.

Right: The Norvic Cinema on Prince of Wales Road. It was opened on Boxing Day 1912, as the Electric. The cinema was modernised in 1949 and became the Norvic. It closed down ten years later, in 1959.

Below: 95-110, Prince of Wales Road looking towards the bottom of Rose Lane. Delves Motors Ltd, on the corner, sold Vauxhall Cars, Bedford Trucks and Scammell Articulated Vehicles.

The Great Eastern Hotel on Prince of Wales Road, being demolished in 1963. On this convenient site the Hotel Nelson was built. It is now a Premier Inn.

The Railway Station on Thorpe Road. The first station was built in the early 1840s when the railway arrived in Norwich. The station shown here was built in 1886.

Norfolk Scenes

George Plunkett often went further afield to take photographs of Norfolk buildings that were rapidly disappearing. Above, is a picture of **Bawburgh Hall**, which was built for the Jerningham family and stood from 1634 to 1963.

St Wandregesilius Church in Bixley - a 13th century church destroyed by fire in 2004.

The ruins of **Costessey Hall**. The original E-plan house had impressive alterations made to it between 1826 and 1836, also for the Jerninghams. Sadly, only the belfry remains.

Above: The Dutch Pier at Gorleston on Sea. It dates to the 16th century. A year after this photograph was taken in 1961, a new pier was built to replace the one seen here.

Left: The Flint House and Drury House on the South Quay at Great Yarmouth.

The old Bure Road Bridge, leading into Yarmouth centre, was replaced in 1972 with a new one.

The fountains on **Marine Parade**.

The Octagonal House on Yarmouth Road in Thorpe St Andrew.

The Westwick Arch and Dovecote which spanned the North Walsham Road until it was demolished in 1981.

Above: The original Cock Inn on the Drayton High Road, which stood here from 1836 until 1956.

Right: A water pump on the Newmarket Road, Cringleford. It was erected in the early 19th century and was used to provide water for road-making.

Right: The Ruins of St Lawrence Tower and the east end of St Mary's Church in South Walsham both date to the 14th century. The tower collapsed in 1971.

Left: The church tower and spire of St Andrew's Church, Thorpe. The scaffolding is in place because of repair works which had to be carried out after the church was bombed in the Second World War.

Index: